FIRE

How to create a complete passive income strategy

By Neil Caine

Contents

Preface

Have you ever imagined how great it would be to be able to earn a good amount of money while putting in the least amount of effort once you retire? To many, the idea might sound too good to be true, but let me tell you that it's achievable. The main way to do this is by creating a passive income strategy. For those who aren't aware of what a passive income strategy is, let me brief you about it. Passive income is income that you can earn without putting in much effort (you can even earn money while you sleep!). You just need to have a sorted strategy in place, and with that, you can earn a good amount of money. When you retire, it's natural to want to be able to sit back and relax while the money flows in. The one way to do this is by devising your own passive income strategy.

This book will act as your guide to setting up a great passive income strategy. Once you have a good passive income strategy in place, you can sit back and relax while earning a handsome amount of money. How you use this money is then up to you. In this book, I have also provided a lot of personal examples from my own life that can help you relate to the information provided. If you're someone who's looking to have a handsome amount of money flowing in even after you retire, then the best thing to do is devise your own strategy. There most definitely isn't one prescribed way to do this. You need to first recognize what your area of expertise is and then work in that area to start raking in the money.

Introduction

Many years ago, I was asking myself: how do I find more time, more money, more energy in my life?

I had a good job, but in my mind, I wanted to be somewhere else. I couldn't find a way to just walk out through the door in order to feel better, because I needed the paycheck that I was getting each month. However, I couldn't leave because any job that I felt I wanted to do didn't pay enough. I felt trapped. So I continued to do a job that I didn't want to do. But it wasn't bad enough so I tried to stand it, just another period, and yet another period. I tried to change employers and realized that the job at the next place was similar, just another employer and other colleagues, but still trapped.

So I started to search for a solution, I needed to open up my mind to see things from another perspective. I bought books, read blogs, joined seminars, and courses with one mission:

I want to find a way to be <u>Financial Independent</u>.

And my goal was to <u>Retire Early</u>, or at least be able to choose what to do with my time, independent of the paycheck that kept me trapped. The main idea behind this was that I want a life for myself where I can live easily without having a financial crunch and the solution wasn't obvious. I knew what I wanted, but I didn't know the exact way that I would need to resort to in order to get there.

I practiced what I learned. I tried different methods and systems, and I failed, and I lost money, but more important: I lost time. But I failed myself to success, using the learning-by-doing method. The breakthrough was when I realized that one of the

mistakes was to try to find shortcuts, and instead learned to use time as a tool, then things started to move in the right direction. I started to build a <u>Magic Plan</u>, one that actually works.

So, I have earned a lot of experience, both in what works and what doesn't.
When you fail, there is always another option; you just need to find it.
Let's go; let's make a plan! <u>A Magic Plan!</u>

The one thing that you need to understand is that you will have to practice, to do this for yourself. You will have to figure out a way that you think would suit best. That is the key to success.

Target and Vision Board

It is always stronger to long for something than from something. As the mind works regarding visualization, the word "not" does not exist. Let's try an experiment. Don't think of a pink elephant. What are you thinking of? If you're thinking of something you don't want to think about, your mind will naturally gravitate toward what you don't want to have. So, turn it the other way, find out what you want to have, and focus on that.

Like I mentioned before, you need to have your goals right in front of you. When you know exactly what you want, getting there will become a lot easier for you. The first thing you need to do when you work on this is sit and jot down exactly what you want in life. Once you have that, you can easily work your way through it. You should be able to envision yourself as being there (achieving your goals). When you see yourself at a certain point, you will find it in you to work hard to get there.

Once you set your target, the next thing you should do is mind map your path to achieving that goal. You should think hard and come up with different ideas that can help you pave your way to your eventual goal. These ideas that you have to think of won't just come to you the very minute you begin thinking. You need to think long and hard about the different options along with their shortcomings and their benefits. You also have to think about what you are good at and how you will be able to manage these different options. Once you have these in mind, you can set different parameters of measuring out these options. After you have done that, then you can shortlist a few options for yourself.

Are you wondering why it's necessary to have a target and vision board for yourself? Do you think this is an unnecessary step? Well, let me tell you something; it is definitely not an unnecessary step. The one main reason why you must have a target and vision board is that it keeps you motivated. When you see your goals right in front of you, you stay motivated. The importance of being motivated cannot be stressed enough. To be able to achieve something, you need to be motivated to get there and it is only that inner motivation that will keep you working hard to achieve your goal. It will give you that extra push that you need to get what you want.

Another major advantage of having vision boards is that it makes your dreams much clearer. When you know exactly what you want, the way you move ahead with it will be different. For example, 'I want to have more money in a few years' is a very vague vision. These are not the kind of goals I'm talking about here. Your goal should be more like, 'I want to have this much money at this point in my life.' With such a vision, you know exactly what you want and at what point in time in life you want it.

Oprah Winfrey pulled herself out of poverty and is now one of the wealthiest women in the world. She had her visions and goals set straight right in front of her. She was always a great supporter of vision boards. She is known to have said, "My life will not be like this; my life will not be like this; it will be better!" many times to herself. She had her goals clear and she knew how she would achieve them as well.

One of the other major reasons that you need to have a vision board is that it makes you more productive. When you're aware of your goals, you work toward them with renewed energy. Your vision board guides you through the path to take you where you want to be. When times are tough and you feel like you're struggling, your vision board will help you by reminding you of what it is that you want to accomplish and how you can do that.

Before you go to sleep write down the first three things you should do the first thing in the morning, before anything else, and the three things should be something that takes you closer to your target; you will always move in the right direction.

People usually overestimate what they can achieve in one year, but they underestimate what they can achieve in ten years.

The Math Principal

The entire concept of a passive income strategy is based on a simple math concept that you need to fully understand before you make your own passive income strategy.

Say, for example, if you win x millions in a lottery, and suddenly you have a lot of money, which most definitely doesn't make you financially independent. You also need to have a financial education on how to handle it in a proper way. If you're just spending what you have in your bank account, it will be a burn-rate curve to zero. It's just a matter of time till the bank account is empty. Your bank account must be re-filled on a regular basis; it doesn't matter whether it's from active or passive income, to cover your living costs. If you just burn through your money, then before you know it, you won't have any more money to spend.

It's like a cash flow game. You are financially free when your positive cash flow from passive income is bigger than the negative cash flow from your total living expenses. It isn't that difficult to understand, really. Once you put your head to it, it'll be easy to wrap your head around.

Everything is based on simple math. To achieve enough passive income to pay your living costs, you must do the following:

1. Take control of your expenditures. The first is to be aware of them and how much you need to finance your lifestyle. The second is to minimize them. But this is different for different people; some people can live on almost nothing, and some people need a lot of "stuff" to live comfortably. It is entirely up to you. What is a luxury for you might

be a necessity for someone else. So you first need to figure out what your current costs are. Then, you need to figure out what exactly you will be able to cut down on. It is obvious that it's easier to be Financially Independent by passive income if the costs are low. The last step is to implement your strategy to cut down on unnecessary expenditures. You need to understand that you'll definitely have to compromise on your lifestyle in order to be able to cut down on costs. You can't work on the have-it-all principle, because that makes things extremely difficult.

2. You must find money to invest, to create a money-making machine. It can be money from savings or any other form of income. The only way to multiply money is to invest it. You need to do your research to find good avenues to invest in. Only then will you be able to put in your money into something that gives you good returns. Just make sure to do all your background research first. If you are not careful with this at this point in time, then you might also end up losing a lot of money.

Always pay yourself first. Decide a fixed amount or percentage of your monthly payment and send it to a saving account the first thing when the money arrives. Because if you pay for the bills and everything else you need first, you will be left with close to nothing to invest. If you start with sending them away to work for you, you will never count them in as available money for the monthly costs. Try to be aggressive with the level of savings and you will be grateful in the future.

3. You must send the money to work for you. And you must give it time to grow. Patience is key here, and you can't rush things. You need to know that you

won't see your money doing wonders right at the beginning. It will take some time. This is because investments also depend on the condition of the market at that point in time. You might not always see returns coming in when you have just begun. You need to be aware of all the factors that affect the market to make sure you get the most out of your investment.

The Formula

Here is the formula how to live on your stock dividends, and a simplified risk strategy.

Step 1: Work out your annual expenses (E). Or if you prefer your monthly expenses, multiply by 12.

Step 2: Find some high yield dividend stocks. Select high quality stocks on a realistic dividend level (D) and avoid the ones with too high dividend. Max 5-6% annually, if the dividend is higher it might not be long term sustainable. Be sure the dividend percentage of the company's yearly profit is in the range of 30-70%.

Step 3: Put the money (E) and (D) in the formula to see how much money (M) you need to invest in the stock market to be able to live on the dividends.

$M = E/D$

Example 1:

If your total monthly expenses are $2500 you need $30 000 yearly.

Dividends from company A, with the yield 4%:

$30 000/0, 04 = $750 000 worth of stock A

Example 2:

If your total monthly expenses are $2500 you need $30 000 yearly.

Dividends from company B, with the yield 5%:

$30 000/0, 05 = $600 000 worth of stock B

Example 3:

If your total monthly expenses are $2500, you need $30 000 yearly.

Dividends from company C, with the yield 6%:

$30 000/0, 06 = $500 000 worth of stock C

To diversify, you need to spread your risk on a number of stocks.

With examples 1-3, we can diversify the yearly need of $30 000 in thirds.

That means $10 000 for each third.

A: $10 000/0, 04 = $250 000 worth of stock A
B: $10 000/0, 05 = $200 000 worth of stock B
C: $10 000/0, 06 = $166 667 worth of stock C

In total, you need to invest $616 667 in order to get $30 000 in annual dividends.

Of course, you can have more than three stocks, the more, the better. This is just to visualize an example.

Balance Sheet, the Key to the Magic Plan

The balance sheet can give you an overview of your financial situation. It's like a holistic view of where you stand in terms of your finances. You must know how to read the balance sheet properly so that you can be efficient with your expenses. Everything you measure will improve over time. You will see the improvements bit by bit, on the way to your target of being financially independent. One of the major benefits of a balance sheet is that, if you make any changes to your plan of how you are going to work around your finances, you will be able to see all the effects of that on your balance sheet.

The balance sheet essentially focuses on the cash flow. You always start with negative cash flow if you invest in something. It takes time before you see money coming in and before the cash flow turns positive. Every month, you have to pay for your living expenses, food, car, etc.; basically, your living expenses. Everything you need to buy has a cost, a negative cash flow; it takes money from your pocket. So, what is the total cost of your life? Don't cheat; be realistic with yourself! Your expenses might be very different from any other person's expenses because people spend on different things according to their lifestyles and preferences. Having a balance sheet can help you since you'll be able to keep track of your expenses at all times.

On the other side of the balance sheet, you must have a positive cash flow that's equal to or greater than the negative cash flow. And the positive cash flow can be both active and passive. The important aspect here is the passive cash flow, and how it grows. It will be possible to see what percentage of financial freedom you're at. It will trigger your thoughts to try to increase the percentage, to find more and bigger passive income streams. Once you have these passive income streams, your balance sheet will start to show a very positive financial situation. You will essentially be sitting back, doing nothing that requires a lot of your attention or time, and you will see the money flowing in.

Decrease Costs

Decreasing costs is key to being able to sustain a certain sum of money for a longer period of time. You might not be paying too much attention to the fact that there are a lot of unnecessary costs that you can easily cut down on to save more. You will be surprised how much you can cut down on your spending if you take a critical look at your costs, especially all your recurrent costs. These may be such small costs that you don't even notice them, but altogether, they sum up to a huge amount at the end of the month. These can be expenses like cigarettes, coffee drinks, soda, candy, snacks, etc. These also include all kinds of streaming costs like Netflix and Spotify.

Here are a few ways that you can effectively reduce your expenses:

1. Track your spending

    This is highly essential. You should know exactly what you're spending on right now so that you can keep track of that. Once you're fully aware of all your expenses, only then you will be able to cut down on the unnecessary ones. What this essentially means is that you should save all of your receipts and write down your expenses in one place so that you can have a fair idea of how much you are spending. There are also a number of apps that can help you to track your expenses.

2. Divide your expenses

The next thing that you should do is divide your expenses into three categories:

I.   Fixed expenses: these are the expenses that you have to pay every month, and they don't change over time. For example, your rent expenses or your insurance. You can't cut down on these expenses, but you need to be aware of them.

II.   Flexible expenses: these are the expenses that you incur on a regular basis and they are mostly for your necessities. For example, these can include your grocery expenses or your phone bill.

III.   Discretionary expenses: these are your luxury expenses. To explain it better, this is the money that you choose to spend on things that are more like 'wants.' These are the expenses that you can cut down on most. These include buying clothes, going to the movies and so on.

1.   Pay your bills on time

This is something that is very much in your control. You need to make sure that you pay all your bills like your phone bills and your electricity bills on time so that you can ensure that you don't have to pay any sorts of late fees or extra finance charges. Think about it; why would you want to waste your money like that, out of sheer laziness? You can actually save up on a lot of money if you pay your bills on time.

3.   Be a sensible shopper

Before you make any purchase, make sure that you consider your needs. I'm definitely not proposing that you don't buy yourself clothes or other things that you like. What I'm trying to say is that you should make a conscious effort to not indulge in impulse buying. If you go out to shop and you like three shirts, then maybe you could buy one of them and save up on the money that you would have otherwise spent on those two shirts. The one best way that you can do this is by first determining your budget first.

Allot a certain amount that you can spend on shopping and then do just that. Engaging in sensible buying also means doing all your background research first, so that you can get what you want at the lowest possible price. Most of the time, the one thing that you want to buy is being sold at different places for different prices. You need to make sure that you make a smart move here. It's also a great idea to wait for sales to buy things. You can also keep an eye out for coupons and offers to get your hands on the best possible deals.

4. Food expenses

Are you used to eating out at restaurants too much? If your answer to that is yes, then you have a bit of a problem. Restaurant meals can be quite expensive. When you're planning on cutting down on expenses, then be sure to cut down on your restaurant meals, too. When you cook your own meals, you can save up on a very good amount of money. I'm definitely not saying that you should restrict yourself from eating out altogether. All I'm saying that if you ate out twice a week, then maybe it would be great if you could bring that down to twice a month. That would reduce your eating out expenses by almost half! Imagine that. All you need to do is be smart with your approach. Get your specific amount of groceries each month and then work your way around cooking your own meals to save up on hefty expenses.

5. Travel and entertainment expenses

Travel and entertainment expenses fall under the head of discretionary expenses. If you're planning on going somewhere, then you should keep an eye out for ticket prices that keep fluctuating. By getting your tickets on the cheap, you can save up on quite a lot of money every year. You can do this by also being flexible about the days that you're going to fly on. Since weekend ticket prices are high, maybe you could try flying on a weekday, so that you can save some money there.

You can also cut down on your expenses on entertainment. If you go to watch movies twice a month, then maybe you could bring that down to once a month. When you go to watch a movie, you obviously spend on food and drinks as well. So if you reduce the number of times that you go out to watch a movie, then that can significantly reduce your expenses as well.

You could travel around the city on a bicycle since it is cheaper than the most ways of commute. Save money wherever and whenever possible and sent them to work for you, in order to build up your passive income.

6.   Make tradeoffs

You need to know that you can't afford all that you feel like buying. You will have to let go of something to buy something else. Or maybe you could make tradeoffs between activities as well. So, for example, if you have to go out and eat or if you have to go to the movies, then maybe you could choose one of the two to save some money.

8.   Avoid consumer loans and credits

The interest rates works the opposite way; they are someone else passive income. So, just make sure that you don't fall into the trap of getting loans that will eventually have you pay much more. By doing this, you can actually save up on a lot of money.

Definitions, What Is Passive Income, and What Is Not?

Before you start your journey of earning passively, you need to know the difference between active and passive income. Active income is what you earn by physically working each day. It is linked to your time. If you stop spending time on what you are doing, you will also stop earning money from it. It's actually really simple to understand. Your day job is your source of active income. If you stop working, you won't be paid.

Passive income, on the other hand, is the income that you earn without really having to work for it on a daily basis. It just keeps flowing in. It comes from something you do one time, and the income will come to you over a period of time. You definitely need to put some time and effort into maintaining your passive income stream, but it doesn't require your complete time and attention.

Examples of active income include holding an office job or mowing the lawn after work to earn a little bit of extra money. It is such jobs that you do have to show up to on a daily basis to earn from it. If you don't come to work, you don't get paid. It's that simple to understand. You're investing your time and energy in it, and that is how you are earning from it.

The idea of passive income sounds attractive to many, right? Imagine being able to earn without really putting in a lot of time into it. It isn't that difficult. You just need to do a sufficient amount of research so that you understand the different ways that you can earn, and then you can work your way up from there. We've all heard the phrase "work smarter, not harder." That is exactly what passive income is all about. You need to figure out a way to earn money without really having to go to work each day. You might feel tired of working 9 to 5 each day without really achieving much from it. Passive income can help you earn a very comfortable life for yourself, even if you're not doing much in the way of active work.

The one thing that you need to know about passive income is that there are different ways of being taxed on it. Different types of passive incomes are taxed at different rates. You can use different strategies to minimize the taxes on your passive income in order to go big on your savings. Imagine how much you can actually save up by working in the day time at your office and also having various streams of passive income that can help you earn a good amount of money.

Examples of Passive Incomes

There are so many different examples of passive income that you have. In order to find which one is the best for you, you need to do some background research that is very specific to you. There are thousands of opportunities when it comes to passive incomes; some are brilliant, and some are pure frauds. So without going too deep into that, you must try what is best for you; it all depends on what risks you are willing to take, how much money and time you can invest, what experience you have and how skilled you are, what time horizon you have and so on.

Written below are a few of my favorite ways of earning passive income. I'm speaking from my own experience, so all of them might not resonate with you. I've written these to give you a good idea of what passive income mainly entails and also so that you can get a good idea of a few real examples.

These are only a few examples to be used as inspiration; others might have a different view on this.

1. Stocks, and in particular, dividends from stocks. Stocks are a great way for you to earn a good amount of money. When you invest in stocks, you can earn money while sleeping. Come to think of it, you're sending your money to work for you, not the opposite. But having said that, you need to know all there is to know about investing in stocks. Then only will it be able to work successfully for you. Visualize it with a Dividend Tube.

It's like a time tube where the total number of dividends comes to you per year, day, hour, or whatever time you want.

Of course, you won't have much to start with, but give it time and learn how compounding interest rates work for you over time. +15% per year is +100% in 5 years. It will have an exponential curve, which means that it will grow exponentially each year. Re-invest your dividends into new stocks and watch them grow stronger and stronger. Re-invest it until you need it in your retirement plan, some years later, and then start withdrawing from your passive income from dividends.

2. Tenants, rent out a room in your house to a student or buy an apartment to rent it out.

Renting out is essentially the easiest way for you to earn money. If you have any kind of extra space available, then what can be better than having someone use it and pay you for it? You're essentially doing nothing and are being able to earn from it. Start where you are, re-invest, and build up a portfolio. Be patient and let time be your friend. It is not completely passive income, because as an owner, you have the responsibility to make sure that everything works for your tenants, but kind of passive. Or if you have a budget that allows you to outsource the responsibility to someone else, it makes it more passive but gives less income to you. And don't forget to fund a maintenance plan in your budget, so you aren't surprised if some damages happen to your house that are too expensive to account for.

3. Sell everything you don't need, and buy anything that gives a positive cash flow.

Send the money to work for you; they work better on the stock market than in your storage.

4. Family-owned company

It could be passive if you hire all functions, including the CEO, and you stay away from the daily business, as a pure business owner. But then this is, of course, easier said than done. There is no doubt about the fact that being a business owner can make you earn a lot of money, but you most definitely need a lot of spare cash for that, which most people don't have. If you have extra cash to invest, then this is definitely the best thing for you to do.

5. You can join an MLM-business.

Multi-level marketing works for some people, but not for all. A lot of initial work needs to be done, and if you succeed, it can be more passive income over time. But it requires maintenance to stay on top.

6. E-business

You must do an initial job, and if the setup is done in order to have a passive e-business and if it works, it could be kind of passive. However, it requires maintenance to keep working properly over time.

Take a look at e-business with drop-shipping that means you can ship goods without having it on stock. When you sell something at your e-business the order will go direct to the producer who will ship direct from the producer to the customer without passing your hands.

Or e-business with selling e-products. The customer pays and then download your product. You can make an e-product once, and then sell it again and again. And it all on remote, you set up the e-business and the customer do the rest.

7.   Royalty from music, books, video games, etc.

You do the job once, and every time someone buys your product, you will be paid royalty fees. Such a great idea, right? If creating music is your passion, then this is a great way to put it to use, and also, of course, earn from it.

8.   Commission anything.

It is based on a cash flow that gives you a share of the payment, sometimes once and sometimes continuously, depending on the business model.

9.   Buy something to rent out.

A caravan, tools, a boat, a parking lot, etc. But then again, you need to have some extra cash available for this. It does not necessarily have to be your own cash. Think smart and find a solution.

Just an example: Maybe you should try to find a business partner? You have a smart idea, your business partner has some money. You start up something together and share the profit 50/50. And you will get passive income without having the money to invest in it.

You need to learn how to calculate returns on investment, ROI. You can buy it with cash if you have it available. And you can use OPM (other people's money) as well. You can also borrow if you have some amount of money missing. You could try borrowing from a family member, a wealthy friend, or the bank.

Here is a simplified business model: what is your ROI if your deposit share is 20% and the bank's is 80%? It will be 5x leverage on your deposit, minus the cost for the interest rate to the 80%. 10% vs. 90% gives 10x. If the initial ROI is 10% and the leverage is 5x, you will have a leveraged ROI of 50% on your own money, minus the cost for interest rate.

Of course, there is a higher risk to borrow. If it goes bankrupt, you will have nothing left but the debt for the 80%. But if you know what you're doing and are willing to take the risk, the leverage will give you a higher ROI. This strategy is also applicable for the stock market, to use leverage on your stock portfolio.

The target to only live on passive income is big. An elephant is also big. How do you eat an elephant? Bit by bit. Move forward step by step. Don't try to take shortcuts. If you do, you will most likely lose both money and time. There are a lot of scams out there, so don't try to save time and make yourself financially independent in an unrealistically short amount of time. There are, of course, examples where somebody has succeeded with an idea, but there are more examples where people have failed when they are desperate to earn quick money.

Here are a few examples of not-so-passive means of earning income, in my opinion:

1. Trading, like stock trading, forex trading, crypto currency trading, etc.

This is extremely high-risk if you aren't sure of what you're doing. Even if it works, trading on a daily basis is not passive. If you stop with the trading, the cash flow will also stop. It is more like a job where you're going to work; you're investing a lot of time in this.

2.   House owner with tenants.

If it is a small house and you have to do everything on your own to please your tenants, it's not passive. If you stop what you are doing, your tenants will move away after some time. It is a job to take care of a house with tenants.

3.   Small business owner.

You run your own business, but the business depends on your presence. It is not passive; you own your job.

Get a mentor

You can try *some* of the methods above, but you will fail for sure if you try all of them. That is why I'm stressing the importance of doing a sufficient amount of background research first. It will cost you both money and time to engage in the trial and error method by yourself until you find what is best for you.

But the one shortcut that you can take to be financially independent through passive income is by having a mentor. Pick a mentor who you know has already tried a lot and has had a lot of experience in life; a mentor who already is in the position where you want to be. He will be able to guide you best since he has gone through the process that you are now going through. He should be willing to share all his experiences with you so that you can learn from him.

If you have problems finding a physical mentor, then you can find him or her on the internet on blogs, groups on social media, etc. Search until you find your inspiration. This might take some time, so you need to be sure that you are patient with the whole process.

Written below are a few reasons why it is of utmost importance to have a mentor:

1. Mentors provide information and knowledge
Mentors have all the information that you could possibly need. This means that they can guide you in the right direction. In the beginning stages, there might be a lot of information that you don't have or you might be in a very confused state. Your mentor can guide you best with regard to this.

2. Mentors can see where you need improvement
Since mentors are much more experienced and have gone through all the necessary procedures, they can very well see the areas you need improvement in. You can only grow when you improve in the areas that you

lack. Mentors give you constructive criticism, and they also are very honest with all shortcomings. They help you see things in a way that you hadn't seen before.

3.   Mentors can help you grow professionally

A famous movie director has said that "The delicate balance of mentoring someone is not creating them in your own image, but giving them the opportunity to create themselves." This is exactly what I'm talking about here. If you have a mentor, then you can grow professionally really well, with the advice that they give you.

4.   Mentors encourage you

No matter how driven on the inside you are, an extra push is always necessary. Oprah Winfrey stated, "A mentor is someone who allows you to see the hope inside yourself." Whenever you feel low, they are there to make you believe that you can do it.

5.   Mentors are disciplinarians for you

It is very important to have boundaries set for you. Your mentors can do that for you. They can also teach you good work habits so that you can succeed.

6.   Mentors teach from experience

Nothing can teach you the way experience can. Mentors can tell you all about their experiences and what they went through. You can use that to your advantage, and that can really help you on your road to learning.

7.   Mentors are priceless

This means that they act as the guiding light in your life, but they don't charge anything from you. They are priceless in more ways than one.

Increase Passive Income to be Able to Decrease Active Income

When you have a balance sheet with visible income streams, both active and passive, you can play with the numbers to see what happens if you stop working tomorrow. How much is missing? And where can I find it? Can I duplicate the passive income I already have, or can I add something else to it?

Once you have a steady stream of passive income, you can make your life much more relaxed. You don't have to work all the time to be able to earn a comfortable living for yourself. You can significantly reduce the number of hours that you work at your office. This means that you can have a significant number of hours to yourself each day that you can spend doing what you like. Doesn't the idea sound ever so enticing to you? Imagine being able to spend more time with your loved ones and being able to go on trips more often. Wouldn't that just be great?

Can I afford to reduce my active hours to be able to spend more time and build up my money machine? Yes, you very well can. Now that you know all about what the different ways there are to earn passive income, just work your way towards it. If you can have more hours free in the day, then why wouldn't you? Consult your mentor, do your own research, talk to your friends, and use your imagination to think of the different possibilities there are that can help you earn a good amount of passive income.

Do you have an extra room in your house that is absolutely of no use to you? If yes, then great. Maybe you could rent that out. Do you have some spare money? Maybe you can invest in stocks or forex. Do you have a good amount of extra money? Maybe you could start some small business of your own. There are so many options for you out there. You just need to think about them and then come up with the best option for you.

One piece of advice for you is that you should start off with a less risky project, where, in case it doesn't work, the chances of you losing money are low. For example, if you're renting out an apartment, then what's the worst that can come out of it? Nothing, right? But if you invest in stocks, without really having good knowledge about it, then that way you really can lose a lot of money. But then, no risk no gain. You just have to find the right balance between risk and gain/reward.

MSI (Multiple Sources of Income)

Have you noticed that almost all wealthy families have multiple sources of income? It is always a wise decision to do so, so that you have different ways of earning. In case something goes wrong with one of them, you have the other to fall back on. These wealthy families know how to spread the risks. Over time almost everything goes up and down in cycles. When the stock market goes down, something else goes up. Maybe other commodities like gold, silver, soya beans? Maybe house prices can match when stock prices are falling?

Written below are a few reasons why you should have multiple sources of income.

Rising health care costs

Health care services are increasingly becoming more expensive and out of reach. That is why it is essential that you have multiple sources of income so that you are easily able to afford health care services.

Paying for education

Education is also now much more expensive than it used to be. When you have multiple sources of income, you can easily afford the best kind of education for yourself.

Pay debt

If you have ever taken any loan and you need to pay it off, then you will easily be able to do so when you have multiple sources of income.

Build a holiday fund

Who doesn't like to go for a holiday or take some time off, right? With multiple sources of income, you can easily do that.

The most relevant of all with regards to passive income is that with multiple sources of income, you can easily earn without really having to go to work each day. The previous chapter talked about having to increase passive income and decreasing active income. That is exactly what you can do when you have multiple sources of income.

For example, you can be trading in Forex or stocks. Alongside that, you can also rent out a space that you aren't using. When you do all of this, you can easily earn a good amount of money, right? You need to realize that when you are working with passive income streams, there are chances that you might make a loss too. So when you have multiple streams of income, you have something to fall back on, and that is the best part about having multiple sources of income. You can easily spread the risk over different sources.

Having multiple sources of income is more like having a safety net. You aren't solely dependent on one way of earning, so in case if something goes wrong, you can easily rely on other sources. Having multiple streams of income can also allow you to be able to use that money and earn much more. When you have money coming in from many different sources, you are easily able to invest and earn more from that.

Act, Make Mistakes and Learn From Them...

The key to earning a good amount by having passive income streams is not being scared of making mistakes. You can make mistakes – it's all part and parcel of the entire game. If you don't act, you will achieve nothing more than what you already have. So if you want to change something and get better results, you must do new things or do what's tried and tested in another way. You won't know whether something will work until you try it out.

What definitely is in your hands is learning from those mistakes. The best lesson that you can learn is from your mistakes and failures. If you repeat the mistakes and don't learn from them, you will also get the same results as before. Don't be afraid of failing. Most people who have gotten success over time have failed themselves to success. But this is only possible if you try, fail, and learn from the mistakes.

Here are five ways you can learn from your mistakes and turn them into valuable life lessons.

1. Acknowledge your mistakes
The first step here is to be aware and acknowledge your mistakes. You will only be able to progress if you do this first. You need to first take responsibility for it, and then you will be able to build up your way from there.

2. Ask yourself tough questions
Grind over why it happened in the first place. Only then you will be able to come up with plausible explanations about the problem. The key is to reflect on the failures. Only then you will be able to be more productive about it.

3. Make a plan

Have a plan for yourself about how you are supposed to go about this in the future. Just know what you are supposed to do when something goes wrong. That can help you a lot. If you keep beating yourself up about the mistakes that are already made, then you won't really get anything out of it.

4. Make it harder to mess up
When you have a good plan in place, the chances of you messing up become much harder. Just have things sorted out and make sure that you do all your research so that nothing can then go wrong.

5. Make a list of reasons about why you wouldn't want to mess up again
When you have a list of reasons as to why you don't want to make the same mistakes again, you can become much more self-disciplined. When you have all those reasons to not mess up right in front of you, you work even harder to ensure that nothing like that happens.

...and Follow Up

Celebrate Your Victories

You may try numerous times, and you may fail numerous times, but as I mentioned earlier, *NOT* giving up is key here. No laws and theorems in science were ever devised on the first try. If these great people had given up, we wouldn't have any science books to study today.

You won't know what works for you unless you *try*. However, if you keep at it, a point will come when things start working out. You will be able to see through clearly and hence, will be able to take your efforts further. If your passive income strategy starts settling in place, you may think *this is it,* when, in reality, this is the point where you need to be all the more vigilant.

A passive income strategy revolves around a number of factors and all these factors together play a role in making or breaking the strategy. Some of these factors are variables while some are not. While you cannot play around fixed factors, you always have room to experiment with variables.

Let's say you have a passive income strategy in place, and it actually seems to be working. What now? Do you stop working on it further and let it work at the pace at which it is currently moving? Although passive income is meant to produce a steady stream of income, a solid strategy is one that not only brings in the money but also increases the income with time!

The first thing that you need to do when your passive income strategy seems to be in place is *analyze* – analyze which factors are playing the most important role, what factors can be worked on further, what factors have the least contributions, and the factors that can be incorporated to make a significant difference.

Once you have that data sorted, you need to follow-up on your strategy and how it's performing along its way. Is there a drop in income over time? Has the income seen a boost at some point? What was the impact on the income when you altered a factor or two? Following-up is extremely important. You need to revisit your passive income strategy regularly to make sure that you don't miss out on any opportunities and also to ensure that your complacency doesn't come in the way of the income growth curve.

If you observe that something that you did along the way gave good returns, never hesitate in repeating it — repeating a process that has worked for you once is never a bad idea. Repeat process also allows you to polish your strategy and become a pro at what you're doing. For example, if you invested in stocks at a particular time of the year and got massive returns, investing in stocks at a similar point in time, considering all external factors, might work for you once again! Also, the second time you're doing it, you will already be aware of things that you were not aware of the first time.

Being financially independent gives you a sense of freedom. If you're a person who works 9 to 5, you know what I mean by 'feeling trapped.' There is nothing that you can do your way; you have to abide by what you're being told, follow a set SOPs every day – much like a robot! All this for the paycheck that you get at the end of the month.

When you have a steady flow of income besides an active income, you will feel a lot less trapped. You will know that if you decide to quit today, you will still have a way to meet your expenses. You won't feel obliged to work for someone else. Instead, the option of quitting will always be there for you. This is the freedom I am talking about.

As you polish your passive income strategy, the inflow will improve too. I am not saying that this will happen over time. After you have crossed the first barrier of cracking a successful passive income strategy, you will now find yourself struggling to cross the second barrier, that is, sustaining the strategy. This is only possible if you analyze your strategy closely, keep follow-ups, and strive to improvise the passive income plan with time. After you cross this barrier, too, you are now en-route to freedom!

The harder you work on making your strategy stronger, the greater freedom comes your way. With greater financial freedom, you will be able to explore possibilities and opportunities because you will know your back is secure, and there is nothing to lose!

Celebrate Your Victories

Whether it is a 9 to 5 job, a self-owned business, or a passive income strategy, one thing is constant, and that is motivation. The day you fall short on motivation is the day you will stop trying to do better. To keep yourself motivated, always make sure you celebrate your achievements regardless of how small or big they are.

To help you understand the effect of celebrations on motivation, let's look at an example. You are an employee at a firm, and you've been given a monthly target. You work hard all month long and manage to achieve it. Do you feel happy? Of course, you do. Do you feel proud of yourself? You probably do. But do you feel like you have made an important accomplishment? You might think that others had bigger targets and they managed to achieve them too, so it's not that big of a deal, right? Well, what happens when your colleagues celebrate your achievement? You will feel like you have achieved something big instantly, and with that, you will be motivated to achieve bigger targets!

Celebrations can really motivate you! If you made 50 dollars with your passive income strategy, celebrate. Instead of telling yourself that $50 is no big deal, tell yourself it is still something you achieved without working for it. Tell yourself that if you can make $50, you can also make $500! Set your next goal and celebrate when you reach there. Instead of setting huge goals that take too long to accomplish, break your journey into smaller parts and celebrate every time you reach the next step. It will keep you motivated!

Celebrating your victories, even if they are small, give you push you need to keep going, the encouragement to move to the next step, and the sense that your achievement is something worth being celebrated.

If you look at your victories, both big and small, as important milestones, you will automatically find yourself wanting to invest more of your time and effort in an attempt to achieve bigger and better things along the way!

Summary

People who are nearing the age of retirement are often seen stressing over how they will manage their expenses and maintain the lifestyle they have had for so long. If you want to stay clear of such stress, you need to start working on the way to generate a constant stream of passive income so that by the time you retire, you already have a considerable amount of money coming in to help you keep going. Having a solid passive income strategy in place long before you retire is the secret to a happy and prosperous, post-retirement, old age!

Knowing that there is an inflow of money in the background not only makes you financially independent but also keeps you from losing your wits over finance and expense management in times of crisis.

Cutting down on unnecessary expenses and putting your valuable money in things that will give good returns over a long period of time is the wisest thing to do if you want to stay prepared for your retirement. If you plan your strategy smartly and wisely, you may even be able to get early retirement and work on something of your own, something that you can own in your name like a small business.

It is important to have someone to advise you every now and then. Your mentor will help you take calculative risks and make smart moves. The constant support and guidance of a mentor, coupled with your smart spending strategy, will secure you in terms of financial standing. It will also make some extra cash available in hand that you can then use for initiating a steady stream of a passive income!

While you may get only small returns initially, staying put and motivated will take you places. There are numerous people out there who have managed to establish passive income streams so big that they don't have to worry about going to work every morning. If you want to enjoy that kind of freedom, start today to reach somewhere tomorrow!

www.ingramcontent.com/pod-product-compliance
Lightning Source LLC
LaVergne TN
LVHW041442170726
843492LV00008B/2763